CADAVERS
AND COCKTAILS

a collection of
true stories
from dark to light

JILL STODOLA

Copyright © 2012 by Jill Stodola

Published in the U.S.A, November 2012
By Jill Stodola
P.O. Box 732
Ortonville, MI 48462
alodotsjba@hotmail.com

ISBN: 978-0-615-69905-9
E-book ISBN: 978-0-615-73264-0

Book design by Lee Lewis Walsh, Words Plus Design,
www.wordsplusdesign.com

Printed by Edwards Brothers Malloy,
www.edwardsbrothers.com

CONTENTS

PART II ☀ LIGHT STORIES

AUTHOR'S NOTE

Cadavers and Cocktails is a collection of true stories from dark to light.
Not for the faint of heart.
The book title is derived from a dream.
In my dream, I was at the morgue with my brother-in-law and sister-in-law.
We were talking to our friend, who is a medical examiner.
He said, "Don't really know why you guys are here. How about we meet after work for cadavers and cocktails?"
Seemed like a novel idea to us.

Dark to Light
To get to the light you must first go through the dark.
The dark part is life's many trials and disappointments.
The light part is when my heart is flooded with happiness.
The happiness is from my victories over problems and a few YES moments.

PART I

DARK STORIES

Eyes Are the Windows of the Soul

People look into my eyes and share the most intimate parts of their soul.

Sexual abuse of children, male and female, by people they trusted.

Stories maybe never ever shared, until their owners met me.

The killing of a man who sexually abused a child, carried out by the grown-up victim.

The story was told to me, in graphic detail, of the abuser begging for freedom.

Under the strong grasp of the victim's hand around his neck, the once-strong abuser was weak.

The abuser was now the victim; he gasped for air as the victim heard his neck break.

The victim took delight in breaking the man's neck and seeing his eyes bulge out of his head.

Finally, justice had been done.

Unfortunately, that was not enough to erase the damage done to this victim.

The damage will last a lifetime; nightmares will continue to haunt this man.

He told me he is not happy unless he kills something every day.

If he had his way, he would live in solitude, in the wilderness.

When I was in fourth grade, a friend told me she went to work with her dad on Saturdays.

Her dad was teaching her how to kiss.

I thought that was odd; I didn't know who I should tell.

When we were in high school, he was found murdered in his car.

Someone had killed him execution-style, with a bullet to his head.

Justice was done, yet the damage to her will last a lifetime.

A friend of mine was married to a Vietnam vet.

He took her out for an evening drive of terror.

When they got to their destination, he blindfolded her and took her shoes.

He left her in the woods and warned her to not tell a soul.

She found her way back and told the police. She divorced him.

I have heard of family secrets not yet divulged, the families sworn to keep "the secret."

Violent Dream

I killed a delivery man.
What was the reason for this violent crime?
I didn't really know anything about him.
Did he attack me?
Don't know.
I took a pair of tarnished wire cutters and repeatedly stabbed him!
Blood spattered everywhere!
All over his guarded cargo!
On my lips, I could taste his salty blood.
I was dripping with his blood.
Too bad; he should've been more careful.
This was all in a teenage girl's dream.

Where Were You?

Where were you on that September morning?
I was safe at home, ironing my husband's dress shirts.
The TV news of the 9/11 attacks shocked me!
This can't be happening!
Not here in America!
Called my husband, was he safe?
Yes, he was safe at work in Auburn Hills.
Were my daughter and son safe?
Yes, both at school under lockdown.
Our country was stunned and in total disbelief!
What a horrific event, so much panic and destruction.
So many lives lost or changed forever.
I can't even imagine the nightmares of the involved families.
There have been great books written about 9/11.
One book talked about all the people who were late for work.
And they were spared from dying in this ghastly event.
Someone had bought new shoes, had blisters and stopped for a band-aid.
In that time, the towers were brought down.
If you are ever sidetracked or delayed, know that there is a reason.
Don't get angry, just go with the flow.
We never really know God's plan.
So many lives lost, so many lives changed.
Every year the 9/11 anniversary stirs up deep American emotions.
All those people who died will never be forgotten!
9/11 was a wake-up call for our country!
Take action, be strong!
Protect the greatest nation in the world!
We must not ever give up!
Never, never, never!
This is now a constant thought!
Where were you?

The Disease

The disease wrecked your body.
The experimental medicine did not work!
While you were sleeping, one of your doctors drew me away from your side.
He told me it was "a little late in the game" to administer that drug.
His words cut like a knife straight to my heart!
A young medical student's jaw dropped in disbelief at his comment.
I had to walk away.
I walked down the sterile halls and wished I could pack a punch!
Because that doctor would be down for the count... or longer!
What kind of thing is that for a doctor to tell a vigilant wife about her sick husband?
I'm sure he was just trying to not give me false hope.
That evening as I drove my hour drive, I had him removed from your case.
His peers were stunned by his lack of compassion.
That medicine made you lose your silky brown hair.
Our daughter said that her daddy's hair was missing.
I told her it was okay and we would get you new hair.
The disease took away your skin. It peeled off in sheets.
Your eyes were sore and bloodshot.
We added salve to soothe the pain.
Your mouth was full of white thrush.
We swabbed it with a numbing medicine to reduce the pain.
Your intestinal membranes were destroyed, blocking any absorption of nutrients.
You had blood transfusions every other day.
The disease halted all blood production.
We thought you were bleeding internally.
Five months after you passed away, we found out the real reason.
It was all part of the disease, GVHD.

Your fever was off the charts; your body could not respond to the fever-reducing medicine.

So they covered you in a seafoam-green plastic cooling blanket.

For a time, the blanket reduced your inferno-like temperature.

You became neutropenic, which means your white blood cells were nearly gone.

They put you on a non-fresh diet to avoid bacteria from plants.

What about bacteria from the hospital?

The diet was so strict that you could not have black pepper.

They warned me not to kiss you, for fear of bacteria.

Looking back, I wish I had ignored their rules and kissed you!

A few of the things we learned from you: fight the battle; maintain your integrity and your sense of humor. Be confident, outspoken and positive.

Loneliness

Loneliness: no one can change it.
That deep, deep blue sadness of death.
It is compounded by holidays, birthdays, and other milestone
events.
You are not here physically to celebrate with us;
I know you are here spiritually.

This Side of Sixty

When I met him he said, "I will be dead this side of sixty."
Wow! That's a real icebreaker of a comment!
He said, "My son will be okay. I will leave him plenty of money.
I'm not taking care of myself. Not ready to change my lifestyle."
How tragic! I know his son and he would really love to spend time
with his dad.

Protective

My parents are now gone, and yet there are still people looking out
for me.
These are people of all ages, both genders.
Some days, I feel too boxed in.
Like I just want to cave in!
I do what needs to be done for family and community.
I just need some space to be me.
Just to spend time with people of my choosing.
Not to be scolded like a child, because I'm making a bad choice!
It's part of my life's journey.

Squirm!

You delight in watching people squirm.
You are excited by their panic.
You always disappear to the bathroom minutes before the plane boards.
Leaves me wondering: should I board or not?
If I go to the bathroom at the bar or restaurant, will you be there when I return?
You are a pro, trying every way to keep me under your thumb.
You play on people's fears and laugh when you win.
Now it's your turn to squirm!

Walk

Get the hell away from him!
If he talks the talk
Sooner or later he'll walk the walk.
Big Red Flag, Hon.
Send that boy packin'!
Walk.

No Explanation

You introduced me to your friends and you told me I was "a good fit in your life."
I got along well with each and every one.
They made me feel like I was "one of the gang."
Your friends told me that since we met:
You are not so angry.
No explanation.
A woman friend said, "it's good he met someone who understands him."
No explanation.
A guy said, "Oh, you're driving him around now."
No explanation.
Now I'm wondering: what did they mean?
No explanation.

Forget About Your Deceased Husband

At first, I looked at all the good times that my new friend and I were having together.

My new friend and I seemed to be a perfect fit.

But now I have opened my eyes!

My friends all told me this was not Mr. Right and that I should run far away!

I didn't listen to them or to my inner voice.

I was having too much fun—or was I?

He used to tell me to forget about my deceased husband, to move past my loss.

He wanted to be the center of my world.

For a time, that worked.

I allowed my new friend to devour my days.

He told me to remember him one day the way I remember my late husband.

He will never be remembered the way I remember my husband.

Friends Say

Before we were dating, they said: *Run Forrest Run.*
The guy is a control freak!
Just by his requests–sight unseen.
People who meet him say he is a good guy.
Up for an adventure, I did not listen.
No regrets, not all bad. Now it is *ugly.*
Friends Say:
He is dangerous.
Get a PPO–personal protection order–against him.
You deserve a hundred times better.
From the outside looking in, my opinion:
You are in danger and if he is around your kids, they are too.
There is nothing normal about wanting sex with a child.
(He thinks twelve- or fourteen-year-old girls would be OK.)
People go to prison for even having pornographic pictures of children.
It's time to walk.
Friends say:
He is darker than dark.

Left or Right?

He said to me:
"I haven't hit you yet–
Do you want the left or right eye?
Maybe punch you in the nose?
You have a big nose.
No breakfast in the morning.
I'm too stressed! You know how I get–
Like Dr. Jekyll and Mr. Hyde.
Guess I shouldn't have said that."
He upsets me with his threats.
One minute we are laughing
As if we are the best of friends
And the next minute,
He asks: left or right eye?

Betrayal of Innocence

I have ignored the weird remarks for fourteen months.
Now they are *boiling* in my brain!
My forty-year-old companion has an obsession with young girls.
Not just young like in their twenties, or eighteen-year-olds, but girls as young as ten.
His extreme honesty is sometimes appreciated, but not always.
For eight years, he declined to go to a friend's "up north" cabin.
Can't imagine why he would turn down the chance for a party?
Not too busy.
His reason: his friend's daughters were preteens.
He did not want to get caught staring at their developing bodies.
Around the fire, he did not want to offend them with his vulgar language.
He and his friends share a "joke."
What's the best thing about your twelve-year-old girlfriend?
After she showers, she looks like a nine-year-old.
He wanted us to go to Key West,
but then said he didn't need to be enticed by all those sexy young women.
I just did not acknowledge these remarks.
Now my blood boils!
In my eyes this is a betrayal of innocence.

Trust and Truth

My father told me that the truth is short and final.
A lie lives on forever.
My feeling about you is *bad!*
Yet I still enjoy your company.
I'm always drawn to the "bad boy."
With you and some of your friends, I feel out of touch.
I feel disconnected.
Alcohol and some of your friends make you act peculiar.
Why?
Do they create another dimension of your psyche?
It seems as if I don't know you or you don't know me.
The feeling is so weird, it makes me want to leave the room and
come back in.
Just to see if you would change back to the man I know.
We have been together for over a year.
Maybe the truth is: I don't really know you.

His Behavior

His reflection: "This is why I'm divorced and probably why I lost my job.
It's because I speak my mind.
Nothing is spared, *every* detail is told.
I don't hold back.
This is me, I won't change."

Warned!

He said,
"I warned you!
(Before we traveled)
That I was gonna call you
every name in the book!
Yell at you!
All day!
Driving is and will be stressful beyond belief.
Wrong side of the car.
Wrong side of the street.
Wrong side of the world.
"Too bad you are a lousy navigator!
Lucky I didn't give you a black eye or two!"
My question: does it that make it ok?
He warned me!
I guess that was his disclaimer, an excuse for awful behavior.
That was not the worst of it.
It was all the cruel and weird comments that followed.
He laughed with friends and said "she deserved a couple of black eyes."
Now I understand–he is *eccentric!*
Warned!

Control

I'm just starting to unravel fourteen months of being controlled by you.
You invited me everywhere; you didn't want to leave me out.
The truth is, you felt that if you left me out you would lose control.
You filled my very lonely days, extremely well.
Perhaps that is why I was so willing to hang with you.
We had too much in common, too soon.
My personal reflection is an eye- and mind-opening gift.
I took a weeklong vacation with my son; you came unglued.
Upon our return, I decided to leave you.
I learned so much in my week away.
The value of faith, family, friends, and respecting myself!
You tried to control from afar with texts implying bodily harm or the threat of infidelity.
The texts were never "good morning beautiful."
Your texts were *always* threatening or "poor me."
You would text "call me."
When I did, you talked nonsense.
Your control is over. I moved on.

Straight-Line Smile

On many occasions you gave me a straight-line smile.
Looking back, it was tight-lipped, teeth hidden as if you were
hiding something.
That smile was pathetic, creepy, sly and cunning.
You gave this smile when there was impending danger and doom.
As if you were anticipating pain and suffering.
Sometimes, it was sad, as if you were a hurt child.
That smile would showed up when I dropped you off after the bar.
More than once, I came into your home, not sure why.
You gave me the same straight, sly smile in Italy at a streetside café.
The tables were set up on the edge of an alley; my chair was almost
in the road.
A truck was headed for me, so I moved my chair and there was that
creepy smile.
Were you imagining my demise?
One afternoon our friends left the bar on their fast motorcycles.
And you showed that same creepy smile and said, "Hope they don't
have an accident."
In the back of my mind, I thought, *You probably hope just the
opposite!*
I do not miss you or your straight-line smile!

Dream Warning

Over the years my dreams have been a great source of personal insight.
When we were in Ketchikan, Alaska, I experienced a very disturbing dream.
I really wasn't sure how to interpret it.
I dreamt I was bleeding, not sure from where.
Lots of red, red warm blood!
The blood kept coming and I couldn't stop it!
It was my blood!
Why was I bleeding?
I felt okay; no cuts; too old for a period.
Was it symbolic of an emotional bloodletting?
Powered by travel uncertainties and stresses?
Don't know.
But here is where it gets interesting:
Five days later, I *had* an accident!
A fall down a flight of stairs, I was crumpled up,
Knocked out and bleeding from my mouth.
The earlier dream must have been a warning of impending doom.
Heed the dream warnings and listen to your inner thoughts.
They are right on target.

Numbers

5 to 8 minutes upstairs
1 flight steep stairs
12:57 a.m. on 5/27/12
1 personal injury accident
1 person crumpled at bottom of stairs
1 tooth broken
1 bleeding mouth
1 person knocked out
1 large bump on back of skull
1 large bump on right jaw
7 scared guests
1 call to 911
1 person saying "don't leave us" to the injured woman
1 man hitting the injured friend over and over again to wake her up
1 ambulance
1 medical center
1 back board
1 orange foam neck protector
Many doctors and nurses
1 male friend to act as my advocate
1 yellow IV bag, replacing lost potassium
1 more ambulance
1 med flight plane
1 man friend to help
1 more ambulance
1 waiting ferry
1 more hospital
Many more doctors and nurses
Do you have any pain?
1 pain from skull bump
1 shot morphine

Zero pain
3 scans
After 10 hours, released from second medical center
1 cab ride to drugstore to fill Rx
My male friend said, "Don't dwell on your accident.
Don't wreck my vacation."
I would have to say that his days are numbered!
Thankful *my* number didn't come up!

Four Times, Not Five

Thought you were dead.
Too many unexplained situations with limited or no recollection.
What happened to me?
Was I overserved or maybe drugged?
The phrase *thought you were dead* has come up four times.
The first was on November 19, 2011.
I was staying at a hotel , I invited him over.
He met me in the bar, we had drinks.
I ordered what he had, thought it was just a whiskey and soda.
Must have been much more than that!
Had an expensive dinner and we shared a bottle of Australian wine.
More drinks in the lobby.
Went to bed, then the bathroom light started flashing!
I got up, ran to the bathroom, threw up with great force!
He sat on the floor and watched me.
He was amused with the intense vomiting.
Were there pictures taken?
This was human suffering.
Next morning, I woke up and he said, "Thought you were dead."
The second time was on December 27, 2011.
It was the fourth anniversary of my husband's death.
We were vacationing in Portland, Maine.
In the evening we had a nice seafood dinner and I had a Bloody Mary.
I left for the bathroom, came back and the night got worse.
Was I drugged or just trying to keep up with this man's drinking?
More drinks at the hotel bar and back to our room.
I remember going to the room, that's all.
I woke up the next morning and he said, "Thought you were dead."
The third time, we stayed at a castle in Ireland.

Must say I had bad vibes about that place, it gave me the creeps!
I felt an overwhelming feeling of despair and sadness.
We had drinks before dinner and during dinner, and an after dinner drink.
More drinks in the massive great room with another family.
I do not remember going back to the room.
I woke up and again he said,
"Thought you were dead. You probably don't remember but you got sick last night."
Funny, I didn't see any barf towels.
What did he do when I was passed out?
The fourth time, we stayed at a lodge on Prince of Wales Island in Alaska.
We had drinks throughout the day, ate leftovers for dinner and had more drinks.
I got angry with him about another woman.
He told me it was time for me to leave the party.
So, he escorted me upstairs to our room and tucked me in.
Next thing, everyone heard a loud crash!
It was me!
I was crumpled up at the bottom of the stairs
Wearing only a t-shirt and naked from the waist down.
I was unconscious and bleeding from the mouth!
What I do remember is a woman leaning over me with huge brown eyes.
She said, "Don't leave us, don't leave us."
Her mom called 911 and wrapped me in a blanket.
My friend repeatedly slapped me, trying to wake me up.
The slapping and the fall left a long yellow bruise on my neck.
They say I sat up and refused the EMS.
My friend told the EMS drivers that I was drunk.
They told him: never say that again!

Next thing I remembered: my friend saying, "Thought you were dead."
There will NOT be a fifth time.
Done with him!
I'm lucky to be alive!

Unexplained

There are too many unanswered questions.
What really happened in the early hours?
On Sunday, May 27, 2012.
I'm unsure of the exact location.
Think it was at a friend's lodge.
We partied in the early afternoon and evening.
Five drinks.
I was angry at him about another woman.
He put me to bed, so I would be out of his way.
Shortly after I went to bed, there was a loud crash.
The guests went to the location of the sound.
At the bottom of the stairs
I lay, crumpled and unconscious.
Wearing only my shirt and naked from the waist down.
I was bleeding from my mouth and unresponsive.
They thought I was dead.
Unexplained.
Friend wanted to give mouth-to-mouth.
Another friend said, "No, she is breathing!"
I don't remember much.
One thing I do remember:
A woman leaning over my face and saying, "Don't leave us."
They say I sat up and refused EMS.
My girlfriend dressed me in soft blue flannel pajama bottoms.
EMS quickly came to my rescue.
This would be the first of three ambulances.
They took us to a local medical center.
Unexplained.
It is reported that my voice was very drawn out and had an echo
to it.
There was an orange foam half-circle keeping my head straight.

It was taped to my head with paper tape.

I was on a white back board. Thought it was yellow.

The staff took forever!

He went outside for a smoke.

Saw and heard the only doctor talking to the EMS guys.

Unexplained.

The doctor told them that "she will be airlifted off the island for testing.

Her tests will more than likely be negative."

The nurse told my friend that I would have to ask to see the doctor.

He woke me up and I politely asked to speak to the doctor.

Where does it hurt?

The back of my head had a huge goose egg bump...

They gave me morphine.

Not sure if it was at that hospital or the next one.

They told my friend I would need to take a medical flight.

They refused to release me.

That was at 1:20 a.m.?

The second ambulance came at 4:20 a.m.

They brought both of us to the landing strip.

They loaded me onto the plane.

My friend and I slept.

They told him it would cost me between twelve and thirty thousand dollars.

I can't help thinking that someone gets a kickback from pushing a medical flight.

I probably made the newspapers.

The small plane landed and unloaded me into a third ambulance.

The third ambulance was on the ferry.

They took us to Ketchikan and over to a hospital.

Scans were done.

Blood was drawn.

They gave me a yellow IV, to replace my potassium.

I faded in and out.
Large bump and bruise on right jawline.
Right side, bright yellow neck!
I was bruised from head to toe on my entire right side.
Unexplained.
As predicted, scans were negative.
They wrote me an RX for pain and gave me my marching orders.
 I was released to my friend.
I was in a total fog.
Too many unexplained details for me.
I will probably *never* know what really happened!

Toe Tag

Almost toe-tagged me and then *you* would be it.
Much to your surprise, I got another stab at life!

Time

Do you ever feel as if you are running out of time?

Not time to do errands, but time in your life.

Don't wait another day to do what you want to do.

Life is a gift, seize the day!

You never know when an untimely accident may change your world as you know it.

Accidents are only planned in the movies.

I had been careful all my life, staying safe inside my box.

Well, my husband died December 27, 2007 at 5:51 p.m.

We had been married for twenty-four years, not all blissful, yet we worked through our problems.

When he died, a part of me died.

I made the choice to "let myself go." To go and do everything!

No holding back; life can be short and can change in a blink of an eye.

Traveled to Sturgis, South Dakota and rode with thousands of other bikers.

Saw the Badlands, Devils Tower, the Needles, and loads of people of every shape and size.

Made new friends and saw old friends.

Felt the wind and the hail on my face.

Not until I traveled to Craig, Alaska did I have a problem.

I was "overserved" and told to leave a party.

Soon I was escorted to my room by my companion and tucked in.

Within minutes, my life changed, possibly forever.

I sustained a fall down carpeted stairs.

I was knocked out, bleeding from the mouth and unresponsive.

I'm not sure how this will affect my future.

From now on you can bet I will be very selective of my companions.

She Knew

Yesterday, I called the med flight company to ask for my paperwork.

The woman asked if it was for billing.

Me: "No, the paperwork pertaining to my flight on Sunday, May 27, 2012."

She said, "You want your transport and medical records."

Me: "That's it."

She asked why.

I told her I wanted to establish a paper trail of events.

She said, "Because you were unconscious, that's understandable."

Her words made me feel numb.

They gave me a sinking feeling.

So much had happened to me, I just didn't have a clue.

I did not remember the flight or the people that watched over me.

Nor do I remember the two hospitals, three ambulances, and a ferry ride.

I thought maybe I had been sleeping.

But no, I was unconscious!

Someone else knows what I don't know.

Now I'm trying to put together the pieces.

My friend said they loaded me on the plane and he went to sleep.

I told the woman that they must have taken good care of me, because I'm here.

She was sincerely happy to talk to me.

She thanked me for saying thanks.

Brain Burn

Your words are burned into my brain.
"You ever harm me, I *will* harm you."
I asked, "Have I harmed you?"
Your response: "Not yet."
What does harm entail?
Does it change from day to day?
You are *not* in control.
A dream vacation, and you spewed this trash from your mouth.
Next trash from you: "If there is a fourteen-year-old girl who owns a yacht,
I'm going to have sex with her. I'm pretty sure it's legal in France."
Weird comments for a man in an exclusive relationship!

Believe

I so desperately wanted to believe you.
Give you the benefit of the doubt.
You walked to the bar, drank too much and the bartenders gave you
a ride home.
You invited them into your house to talk, get into their head and
hopefully into bed.
You told me over and over that it was just for conversation.
Then you told me you would like to bend one over and have sex
with her.
Your honesty is breathtaking!
My guy friends told me that you have an ulterior motive in mind.
I didn't want to believe my tried-and-true friends.
I was dumb. I needed to believe them and not you.

Questions

You always insisted that I drink with you, and even got angry if I didn't.

My girlfriend asked me *why did he want you to drink?*

What was his motive?

He knows you are not a big drinker.

Often you bought me a bottle of wine, and sometimes you had a couple of glasses.

My mistake was that I tried to keep up with an alcoholic.

What was I thinking?

After a while I refused the bottle of wine.

Then you moved onto more intense drinks that were sweet and alcohol-filled.

You claimed the sugar gets the alcohol into your system quicker.

So what!

Why?

I never asked you why you wanted it to be quicker.

In my eyes, you had come to be sinister and suspicious.

You were clearly not my kind of guy.

Even then, I thought of you as Mr. Wrong.

Why did I stay?

Because we had fun; you filled that lonely void in my life.

What did you do when I was passed out?

Did you feel victorious?

She lost, I won!

Did you take pictures of me?

Steal my identity?

Wear my clothes?

Psycho

In the days to come,
He will call me a psycho bitch!
Many people who know me will say that he is wrong!
It is because he lost at love.
Here come the mean remarks, blackmail and revenge.
Who is the real psycho?
Time will tell.

Negative

Yesterday felt like fall because the day was crisp.
You could have been at your son's soccer invitational.
Instead you chose to muddy my name.
You went to four different bars, bad-mouthing me.
You showed my nude pictures to all the patrons. How immature.
Then you were thoughtful enough and texted me what you had done.
I did not harm you, I ended a toxic relationship.
Taking care of me, and no longer taking care of you.
Grow up! Spend time with your son!
He is only young for an instant.
Be a good role model.

Headaches

My headaches are a daily reminder of my accident.
I think it is God's way of driving home the point about my bad choices.
It was a bad and pointless choice to try to keep up with an alcoholic's drinking.
It's been over three months, and the pain continues to haunt me.
Was it an alcohol-induced seizure that caused the accident?
What I do know is that I learned a lot from the whole experience.
It is crucial to know your drinking limits.
Do not waver or allow others to entice you to drink more.
Serious damage will occur to you and all others involved.
Always take your drink with you to the bathroom.
Never be too trusting of a boyfriend or other friends.
This is to avoid possible insertion of date rape drugs in your drink.
Accidents can happen.
I view the daily headaches as a reminder and a blessing.
I feel very blessed to be alive!

Comments

When I first met him, he told me he "will die this side of 60."

What a grim comment for a first date.

Was he reaching out for help?

Judging by the past fourteen months, I'd say that he is right on target.

Not much interest in life.

He is always focusing on the next drink or the next chew.

He has established a course of personal destruction.

Most days, he drinks a case of beer.

Hello, that is twenty-four cans. And then he mixes it with smokeless tobacco.

He seldom eats or sleeps.

Is this depression?

Why doesn't his family see this problem and act on it?

This is a tragic situation which could be avoided.

PPO

Personal Protection Order.
Never knew what that meant.
Now I do.
My sister said to me that I have the right to end a relationship.
I ended a fourteen-month so-called relationship.
We had so much in common.
But months down the road, his true colors appeared.
Very controlling, he made strange comments to me, about other
women both young and old.
His sole purpose was to keep me "under his thumb."
Sad to say, it worked.
Those comments instilled fear in me.
Fear of his cheating and going out with younger women.
Fear of his leaving me or causing me bodily harm.
These threats weighed me down, as if I had an anvil on my back.
Yesterday, I ended the relationship.
He was surprised and confused.
Today, I submitted a PPO request.
Plus a police report.
The deputy did not think he had enough info for a report.
I just want a record of his behavior on file.
Once lovers and now *nothing!*

Toxic

Our romance has turned toxic.
I can't help but think that standing my ground could cost me my life.
I pray that is not the case.
Just got off the phone with the officer who is handling my complaint.
He talked to you and you told him you were trying to work things out with me.
He said that is odd since she refuses to talk to you.
The officer said that is too late to charge him with abuse.
He asked what I wanted done; I said just a written domestic abuse claim.
I need to establish a paper trail.
The officer asked, "Do you want him to continue calling and texting you?"
No, I want him to stop!
That toxic relationship is over.

Toxic Waste

Our relationship has turned to toxic waste.
I envision it as a huge dark, black barrel bursting at the seams
with a large skull and crossbones.
Filled with sadness, cruel threats and uncertainties.
I gave you my best, yet every day you played on my insecurities.
You are the Master of the Game.
If you wanted someone else, why didn't you leave?
Why did you stay?
Each day you spoke of other women's bodies.
"Her tiny butt would look great with your boobs, and then you
would be smoking hot!"
From the beginning, we talked about everything and anything.
Sometimes, I don't need to hear how you crave other girls or
women.
It is absolute disrespect!
When I called you out on it, you told me to get over it!
You told me that's how you are and you will never change.
You told me to hang with you.
I'm done hanging with you!
The damage is done!
All these thoughts are toxic waste!

Gag Order

I'm thinking that I need to have a "self-imposed gag order."
Just so I stop spreading our toxic waste.
How can a relationship go so wrong?
Maybe it's all the threats you have made?
Your friend was quick to point out that I bring it on.
He said you drink more since you met me.
Here is what happened since you met me:
Your new car was hit by a deer.
You lost your phone in the Atlantic Ocean.
You lost your job of 20 years.
Your friend died.
Dog ate your homework. Oops, wrong decade!
I'm feeling like this is the good ol' boys' club coming out.
You are quick to blame others for your problems.
Aren't we all?
We all have been through some devastation.
Your friend said you have had a hard life. It is all how we handle
things.
You would be happier if you made the effort.
Make a change in yourself and stop drinking.

Really?

On trips you told me how carefully you chose me as a travel part-
ner.
Really?
I don't trust your words.
In the next breath you say: "I should've invited the girl next door.
She would've taken it all in."
Really?
"Travel would open her eyes, get her out of her room and into the
world."
Really?
Did it ever dawn on you that travel did the same thing for me?

No Tears For You

There will be no tears shed for you.
Period!
You said *someday when we part, just part peacefully.*
I did, you did not.
You were out of town on an island.
I was at a bar with our friends.
Now I'm the bad guy, because I chose to end it via a text.
"We've had our fun. Now I'm done."
Maybe I should have called you and said it's over.
The outcome would remain the same.
I ended our fourteen-month toxic romance on Monday, August 13, 2012.
You still send nasty texts and threats.
You messaged me that you showed all my nude photos to everyone at our favorite bars.
And that I lose.
What do I lose?
They said I can go to hell.
You are wrong, you lose.
You call me using fake numbers, trying desperately to regain control over me.
You're very clever; you faked a number with my best friend's California area code.
I mistakenly answered it, heard your voice and promptly hung up.
I will *never* talk to you again.
You have been banned from my life!
If you show up at my door, the cops will be called!
You are not welcome anymore!

PART II

LIGHT STORIES

About Me

I have an extraordinary connection to people
and the ability to feel their sufferings.
People seek me out.
They want to spend time with me.
They want to share their day, their sorrows and their joys with me.
People find a certain calm and comfort in my presence.
A young black man said to me, "Girl, your smile could melt three winters!"
It is service before self.
I'm a gentle soul, an old soul.
My purpose in life is to listen, encourage and help.

My Calm

Friends have told me I have a certain peace about me.
They say I have the ability to soothe them and decrease their panic attacks.
Simply by being me, just in their presence.
No conversation needed.
Just sit and listen to their life.

Friends

I have been given the ability to make friends easily.
They can be young or old.
I'm a friend to all, girls, boys, women and men.
I'm eager to hear their stories, really willing to listen.
I'm well-received, as an immediate friend.
What an awesome gift!

My Purpose

Once you know your purpose, your life will gain meaning.
My purpose: listen, encourage and help.
The purpose provides a solid foundation for my two businesses, my book and my volunteer work.
The first business is Friends and Neighbors (FAN).
It is a welcome service that welcomes new residents and businesses.
The goal of FAN is to help the new resident make a smooth transition into their new town.
Alodots Time Savers helps you connect all your dots.
It is a professional errand running service.
This allows the client to make the best of his or her time.
I run their errands and they enjoy their family or friends.
The book *Cadavers and Cocktails* is a collection of personal life stories from dark to light.
I feel it is a way to share and help other people in their lives.
My volunteer work is helping people.
I pack care packages for our troops with other volunteers.
Each box is carefully filled with much-needed supplies.
Volunteers bake homemade cookies, snacks, tastes of home.
We provide socks and personal care items.
We write letters of encouragement and thanks.
We want to be sure that the troops know we appreciate them.
I also stand in honor of those that have died for us.
My group attends military funerals, sends off soldiers, and welcomes them home again.
We stand proudly in formation with our American flags, symbolizing honor and respect for the soldier.
I give blood every ninety days to help save lives, and I encourage people to become organ donors.
I view these activities as a perfect fit for my purpose.

I Witnessed Again

A father confided in me about his son's motorcycle accident.
He said the images would be forever burned in his brain.
He was out finishing up his weekly 5K run.
When he saw two of his three sons riding a borrowed motorcycle,
he looked back and really wanted to ask where they were going.
But he did not. That's the image stuck in his mind.
I don't think they even knew.
He ran home and soaked in the pool with his wife.
Within fifteen minutes his wife got a call from the younger son.
There had been a nasty accident.
Apparently, they had hit gravel and potholes, and slammed into a mailbox,
bringing down their bike and sending both of them to the hospital!
After the news he felt as if he was moving in slow motion.
He and his wife somehow got to the hospital and saw their sons.
As parents we are not supposed to bury our children.
 They are to bury us.
I told him that the old will die and the young can die.
His sons did not look the same.
The younger one suffered less physical damage.
The older one suffered more damage.
The younger son was vigilant and slept by the older son's bed for a week.
The accident has been a true test of God's love and mercy.
This accident has brought the whole family closer together.
Each member is much closer to God.
The father said they don't know the real extent of the damage–not yet.
The son's right hand can almost squeeze a ball.
His story was eerily familiar; another couple's future son-in-law had borrowed a motorcycle.

Took a curve too fast and lost control of the bike.
This was on a back road; his bike flipped down a wooded
embankment.
His parents found him a day later, dead.
I just met the father and he told me this story.

You and I

You and I were raised the same way.
We were raised to act like nothing is wrong when everything is
falling apart.
We were taught not to wear our emotions on our sleeves.
We are of Danish, Finnish, Norwegian and Scottish
descent and taught to be stoic.
We must remain strong and independent.

BYOB

BYOB used to mean *bring your own bottle.*
But now, it means *bring your own book.*
When you bring your own book, waiting becomes a vacation.
Your book will allow you time to escape to your own favorite destination.
Make use of your time to fulfill a fantasy or expand your mind.
A book is always a welcomed escape.

My 52nd Year

A year unlike any other year!
Full of travel and adventures!
The travel started in December with a trip to Portland, Maine.
We stayed downtown, walked everywhere and saw everything.
The weather was unseasonably warm.
We went to all kinds of pubs and ate fresh lobster every day!
We visited an old museum and learned about old Maine.
We drove to Crescent Beach and took pictures in the water.
I accepted a dare to run to a rock in the water.
I had to beat the tide, just in time to pose for a snapshot of me on a rock.
We drove to Boston, just to see what we could see.
In April, we planned a trip to the Republic of Ireland.
We stayed in bed-and-breakfasts throughout the country.
Plush green countryside divided by miles of stone fences.
Made new friends, ate different foods and drank the local spirits.
In May we traveled to Craig, Alaska, to visit more friends.
Craig is located on Prince of Wales Island, which is the third largest island in America.
We took a forty-five-minute flight from Ketchikan to Craig.
It was a breathtaking flight above the forests and rocky shorelines.
We spent time with our friends and experienced firsthand the hardships of catching your food.
They set up crab and shrimp pots on a daily basis, filled with fish heads for bait.
After a stay in Craig, we flew to Portland, Oregon.
There we stayed at a restored school.
The school had been used from 1904 to the 1970s, and then transformed to a hotel.
Thirty-five neatly painted rooms, eight restaurants, bars, a soaking pool and a theater.

It was a unique establishment.
Gardens were filled with flowers and outdoor fireplaces.
We saw my friend's brother and his kids.
I even had the opportunity to see one of my cousins.
After a short time at home, we travelled again.
From June through July, we ventured to France, Italy and Switzerland.
In Paris we saw the Eiffel Tower and the Louvre, and listened to the orchestra.
We stayed a night in Monaco and played in the sea.
We saw many attractions that people wait a lifetime to see.
The weather was absolutely beautiful!
In Italy, we saw the Leaning Tower of Pisa; it's only about six stories high.
We saw the Vatican, the great Coliseum, and Venice, the city of water.
We went to the French Alps and up to the top of Mont Blanc.
He drove like crazy every day, just to go to the next town.
The days were filled with scenic drives and the nights were filled with walking,
We walked five to ten miles every night.
To see what we could see.
No expense was spared!
Everything was paid for by my very generous friend.
Truly a trip of a lifetime!

Thanks For Making The Call

Thanks for coming to my rescue.
You called 911.
You dressed me in soft, flannel pajama bottoms.
Your daughter pleaded with me, "Don't leave us."
A friend hit me over and over again–trying to wake me.
You did not sweep me under the rug.
Nor did you cut me up for bait, to be used in the crab and shrimp pots.
I'm a good-hearted person with much life yet to live.
Thanks for making the call.

Energy

Everything has a place.
Every place has a thing.
Decrease the clutter, mentally and visually.
Then you will feel the empowerment of your energy.

Unknown Life

He died without my knowing him.
Before the eulogy, I knew we shared a few common interests.
After the well-written eulogy, I realized that I should have taken the
time to learn more.
Just sitting and visiting for a mere fifteen minutes could have
opened the door to a fuller life.
Friends of the deceased shared stories of times spent together.
They verbally painted pictures of days gone by.
Stories of hunting, fishing, parties, and well-played pranks.
Their friend's death will definitely leave a huge void in their lives.
But it will also allow their friend's memory to live on in their lives,
for eternity.
Don't wait until the eulogy to learn what you missed.
The time is now. Take time to visit with a friend.
Learn and share their life.

Lines

The marketing company was correct; I don't like the confines of
lines.
I'm not a lined-paper gal.
I need wide open spaces to express myself, in art, in words and in
my life.
Not big on rules or staying in the lines of a coloring book.
I'm very much a free spirit.
No lines, no confines.

Write It Out

Write it.
Express it.
Feel it.
Thought is released.
Draft is tossed in the trash.
Now, I can make room for more stories in my brain.
Thought completed.

Night Owl

That's me; 11:00 p.m. is when I start to hoot!
That is when I do some of my best work on my book and other projects.
I suppose the fact that I was born at 1:01 a.m. has made me a night owl by design.
I often pull all-nighters, writing my best pieces at 3:30 a.m.
I have to make myself leave the limb and head to my nest.
I find it difficult to engage in sleep with so many projects taking flight in my mind.
And then the next day I must endure the consequences of limited sleep.
Forgetting simple things like crossing my t's, dotting my i's and doing math.
Lack of sleep is a small price to pay for this night owl!

Maine 2011

I went to the sea to see what I could see.
A time for me to step back from my life.
Got to live now and not wait!

Going North

Left side of the road is a bar.
It represents a skull and crossbones.
It's filled with feelings of sadness.
It is darkness, destruction and death.
Right side of the road is a coffee shop.
It represents a heart.
It's filled with feelings of caring, love and understanding.
It is lightness.
Share a sorrow and it is halved.
Share a joy and it is doubled.

Crush

The first time I met you, I was like a giddy schoolgirl.
I couldn't wait to see you and didn't know what to wear.
The first time, we talked for three hours; we had so much in common.
I soon discovered that my door was only six minutes from your door.
You made me feel alive!
We both felt so good in our skin.
We talked about anything and everything!
I thought of a question from a high school friend.
He asked me: "What do you want in a relationship?"
I told him: nothing too serious, companionship, great sex and to see him as often as I want.
You fit the bill to a T.
We were so compatible, even though you were eleven years younger.
We are two "old souls;" we have seen much in our lives.
We understood each other.
We ate Chinese food and watched the news.
Late-night chats on your patio over Brazilian drinks.
We enjoyed the same local watering holes, concerts and world travel.
We shared the same sense of humor.
You consumed most of my days and I consumed your days.
You made me feel good about me and I made you feel good about you.

I'm

I'm a daughter without parents.
I'm a wife without a husband.
I'm a mother with two children.
I'm a sister to two sisters.
I'm a cousin, a niece, and an aunt.
They and we are the legacy of lives well lived.
Values instilled at a young age.
We value faith, family, and friends.
Hard work, heritage and a good sense of humor are important to
us.
I'm proud of who we are.

Top Shelf Stories

My therapist said to burn the journals.

Throw them out!

Don't look back!

I couldn't do that.

Those notebooks hold stories of hope, courage, love and integrity.

Not death and destruction.

Those stories are about my late husband Barry, my kids and me.

Top Shelf Stories

I kept them and will continue to keep them.

In the fall, when I'm feeling uneven and down,

I look at the notebooks.

What happened that day?

Those stories are full of hope, courage, love and integrity.

They are very positive.

Because at that time, we did not know that he was dying.

Top Shelf Stories

Well worth the read.

They are full of medical information.

Being his wife and friend, I soon took on a new role of patient advocate.

I made sure that he received the best care possible.

The doctors used to ask him: "How are you doing today, Mr. Stodola?"

He would say boldly, "Just another day in paradise!"

It was that positive attitude that made the doctors try harder.

Try different things to save his life and our life together.

Top Shelf Stories

His sister Amy said *hold onto those stories.*

You may want to write a book.

This book would be all about hope, courage, love, and integrity.

Barry was all about love!

Top Shelf Stories

Why I Do What I Do

Troops:
I pack care packages for the troops, with a group of volunteers.
We pack them in honor of a local young man who gave his life.
These boxes are filled with love, food, and letters of encouragement.
It's our way of giving thanks to those who serve.
Blood:
I donate my blood every ninety days, to those in dire need.
My husband needed blood transfusions every other day.
His body could no longer produce blood.
They said *we are at a critical low, but your husband needs it.*
To date I have given eighteen pints, and there is more to come.
Organs:
I encourage people to become organ donors.
My husband needed a liver transplant.
He ended up having two in one month.
Now, I encourage others to make a difference and become donors.
It's easy, it's painless, and what a great gift to give!
Honor and Respect:
I'm a member of a national organization; we stand for those who
stood for us.
We support local veterans present and past.
With our American flags we stand in a proud straight line.
They stood in honor of my husband.
This is why I do what I do.

FDT 15

FDT 15 stands for first daily thoughts for fifteen days.
When I sleep well, I awake to a first daily thought.
It's a type of personal guidance for me.
I share my first daily thoughts with my friends.
Sept. 5: Gratitude
Sept. 6: Respect yourself
Sept. 7: blank
Sept. 8: Pace yourself
Sept. 9: We will get through this
Sept. 10: Let it go
Sept. 11: Get answers to your questions
Sept. 12: Grover is home. No more bad days
Sept. 13: Are you serious?
Sept. 14: We've been here many years
Sept. 15: blank
Sept. 16: Get up, sit up, take notes
Sept. 17: On the money honey
Sept. 18: Chamomile at bedtime
Sept. 19: No FDT, cat bit foot.
Many of these thoughts are from my daily challenges.
They offer an insight to solve these problems.
Some FDTs are funny or nonsense.
What are your FDTs?

Lena

On a cold, gray November day, I attended a Veteran's Day ceremony.
I parked in the field at the cemetery and boarded a shuttle bus.
Beside me sat a very dignified white-haired woman, dressed in a navy blue wool coat.
Her name was Lena.
We made small talk and discovered we were both widows.
At the ceremony, she again sat next to me.
We shared her blanket, her mints and tissues.
On that cold day, her generosity really warmed my heart.
We both wept when "Amazing Grace" was played on the bagpipes.
The ceremony was bittersweet.
We missed our loved ones and we formed a new friendship.

Aliveness

Today, I woke up with enormous gratitude.
Thanking the Lord for my existence.
Alive!
Thanking for my faith, family and friends.
My girlfriend told me, "I'm happy for your aliveness!"

Happy

Today I saw two friends of ours; the wife told me that I look so happy!
She said that before, it seemed like I had a lot going on in my mind.
I told them it's better now that you and I are no longer a couple.
You are a good guy, but we are bad for each other.
She thinks I'm all better; I told her no, I'm working on it.
I'm home for my kids, being a present parent.
Making meals and cleaning football uniforms.
Writing my book and growing my businesses.
She told me that I will always be special to her.
She gave me her number and two hugs, plus one hug from her husband.
Yes, I'm happy inside and out.

First Name Basis

It's a good touch to name your medical school cadaver.
Not just any name, but their given name.
Every medical student will have a cadaver with their first name.
This will allow the medical students to be more professional.
They can talk to their cadaver as if it were a real patient.
Of course, the cadavers will be the best patients.
They will be cool and calm.

Graveside Coffee

Before my mom passed away, we talked about funerals.
She did not want one, nor did she want an open casket.
The dead never really look like the living.
She didn't want people to remember her as a poorly "made-up"
body.
But if she did have a funeral, it would be simple, with a couple of
favorite hymns.
"The Old Rugged Cross" and "Amazing Grace."
I jokingly suggested graveside coffee.
She liked that idea.
What a great way to say goodbye: coffee at the grave.

Linked to the Lost

What objects, sights, sounds, smells link you to the lost?
Many people have shared these with me.
You never know what will become meaningful.
When someone dies they leave behind memorable personal symbols.
Some of these symbols are:
Dragonfly, ladybugs, hearts, suede moccasins, faded denim jackets, etc.
Favorite songs, movies and lines well rehearsed.
List goes on and on.
They say our loved ones try to contact us right after they die.
But we are too absorbed by our grief to witness their communication.
Now some loved ones are gone.
These memories give us comfort.
And let us stay linked to the lost.

Frogs

I mentioned to a new woman friend that I keep meeting frogs instead of princes.
She told me that you have to really think of what you want in a man.
Almost like choosing a dress.
When you choose a dress, you carefully consider the details.
How you want it to fit, color, length and style.
We spend more time on searching for the right outfit than picking the right companion.
Oddly enough, her office is full of frog figurines and pictures.
Not that she likes frogs; it's what they symbolize.
When water boils, frogs cook, they die.
That's why we need to choose men who are not frogs.
When you meet a man, don't think of it as a date.
Just meet for a coffee or ice cream.
You will know in the first few minutes if he fits your criteria.
If not, move on.
I found out she is a social worker and a life coach.

In a Couple

I'll see you in a couple.
What does *in a couple* mean?
A couple of minutes, hours, days, weeks, months or years?
I think in a couple varies according to context.
It's a measurement of time, sometimes with drinks, miles, places, or things.
I seldom hear kids say *in a couple.*

Hummingbird

I saw a colorful glass hummingbird, suspended on a gold chain.
It was delicate and dangled from a car's rearview mirror.
All I could think was *hmmmmm*.
What hangs from your mirror?

My Parents

I'm so much like my parents.
This is a very positive thing.
I'm learning to witness, like my father.
He was a great and attentive listener.
Dad never judged, he listened, and only offered advice if it was requested.
He took photographs of store openings and promotions.
Camera was always ready to capture a key moment.
He told me it's important to take pictures of people's hands.
The hands are the key to age, at any age.
Both my father and mother were proud of their heritage.
My dad was Norwegian and my mom was Finnish.
We traveled to Norway, Finland, Sweden, and Denmark.
Visited cousins and found out where the relatives had left to come to America.
It was a trip rich in family history.
They liked cooking traditional flavors of their youth.
A few of their favorites were Norwegian meatballs, fruit soup, and lefse.
Mom's Finnish delights were Finnish flat bread and cookies.
I'm much like my mother, fascinated by the human body.
She was a surgical nurse and always shared tales of anatomy.
An amputated leg was sent in a bag to the lab.
She said that it kicked all the way there.
It was the nerves, still kicking.
She had an eye for art, for all mediums.
She could sculpt in bronze, ceramic, and porcelain.
Paint in acrylic, oil, or watercolor.
She too spoke of hands; they are difficult to draw.
When she was in high school she carved a human heart out of soap.
Mom knew how to carve wood, too.

My mother had an ability to play all types of music.
She could play the cello, guitar and mandolin.
Mom played the organ and piano by ear.
In our sunny living room she had a baby grand piano.
She knew and played hundreds of songs!
What a beautiful voice and talent!
They loved singing Broadway show tunes.
The grandkids liked to play "marching band."
My parents let them make noise!
The kids selected musical instruments from a huge bag and made their own music.
I have so many good memories of my parents.
They were great role models!

Simplicity

Is it my Finnish and Norwegian heritage that makes me crave simplicity?
Those cultures make me want to live a simpler life.
Furniture handsomely crafted, with simple yet purposeful design.
Beautiful home furnishings decorated with bold and brightly colored fabrics.
Neatly woven wool rugs accenting hardwood floors.
Wall hangings designed by the home owners, taking in their personal taste.
These furnishings are simple, graceful and unpretentious.
Simplicity is a delight to my Finnish and Norwegian eyes.

Excess

For me, excess is a complete turnoff.
Clutter is mind-boggling.
Who needs it?
My life runs more smoothly when I can put my hands on what I need.
The only excess that I like is when I receive an excess of items to help others.
I will pass on the food, books, clothes and household items to people in need.
Doing what I can to make a difference in someone's life.

Smile

I've been told I have a smile that could melt three winters.
My smile makes people feel comforted and at ease.
Friends say that I'm always smiling.
The way I see it, it's better to smile than to frown.
You are never fully dressed until you slip on a smile.

A Father's Values

He believed in a strong educational foundation.
He had the desire to travel the world.
To know people. Chinese, Russians, anyone and everyone!
It was always service before self.
I still remember his picture with a handful of grants.
Carefully written and received.
His sole purpose was to help others to strive and succeed.
He travelled the world by plane, boat, bicycle, and on foot.
He went to China, Russia, Germany, Japan, Italy and Ireland.
He learned all that he could learn about the people:
Customs and various schools of thought.
If only his bicycle wheels could speak...the stories they would tell.
His suitcase was covered with decals of places he had visited.
He left behind fond memories.
He sent home letters to family and friends.
Sharing his travels and what he had learned.
Have fun before you can't.
Help others if you can help.
But you will never understand.
Go *now* and plant a tree for Dad.
Always remember: education—you must have it!

Thoughts A to Z

Think of this–
Some people pay others for their thoughts:
Analytical
Biological
Creative
Dysfunctional
Energy
Formulas
Geological
Health
Intuitive
Judicial
Kinetic
Lucrative
Meteorological
Nutritional
Original
Predictions
Quantitative
Reflexology
Scientific
Testimonial
Unconditional
Viral
Whimsical
Xenophobia (fear of foreigners)
Youthful
Zoological
So many thoughtful thoughts!

Been There Before?

In the 1970s my cousin and I took a walk.

We saw an old two-story white house with deep green trim.

There was a gray-haired man raking leaves.

I talked to him and told him I know about that white house.

I asked if my cousin and I could go in to the home.

Much to my surprise, he said yes.

I proceeded to share many details of the house with him and my cousin.

The first area was a summer kitchen; it was in the front of the house.

The cabinets were lined with paper in a green ivy print.

Before we got to each room, I told them the décor.

The next room had an ice cream parlor-style table with wrought-iron chairs.

In the center of the table was a lace doily under a vase with one rose.

Lace curtains adorned the windows.

The next room was a living room.

There was a large velveteen couch in front of some French doors.

I told them it is there because he no longer uses those doors.

The arms of the couch were worn off.

In front of the couch was a homemade rag rug.

There was a dark brown Victrola music player and old records.

We went upstairs, where there were two bedrooms.

Each had oversized brass beds, with homemade
dark-colored quilts.

The bathroom had a large white bathtub with claw feet.

The sink was small and had a light over the mirror with a broken cord.

I don't recall the actual kitchen.

He was stunned and asked, "When you were here?"
I was never there until that day.
I don't know how I knew, but I did feel totally comfortable in his home.

Press On

With the human element, much can go wrong, yet much can go on.
There are so many survivor stories.
Everyone has at least one.
The secret here is to press on, beat the odds!
Don't accept NO for an answer.
When one door closes, another one (or two) will open.
Press on!